# BREATHE

For information address:
J2B Publishing LLC
4251 Columbia Park Road
Pomfret, MD  20675
www.J2BLLC.com
GladToDoIt@gmail.com

Printed and bound in the United States of America.
This book is set in Garamond. Designed by Mary Barrows.

ISBN:  978-1-948747-02-8 – Paperback
          978-1-948747-03-5 – Hard cover

# BREATHE

*From the Test to the Testimony Just Breathe "bjai"*

*bjai*

J2B PUBLISHING

# *Dedication*

This book is dedicated to my three amazing daughters
Nicole, Michelle and Jolie,

To these girls who chose to take this journey with me.
"Thank you for always being there!"

# Acknowledgements:

There are so many people who made this book possible;
>   People who made my story a story worth reading.
>   People who were there when no one else even knew there was a story.

>   *This is my journey from mourning to dancing* (Psalm 30:11).

# ⋆ Forward by Lisa Chapman ⋆

When I was approached to write a foreword for my dear and longtime friend, I was immediately taken aback. The mere fact that she entrusted such an honorable duty to me made me nervous and anxious. Am I worthy of such an important task? I have been a writer all my life and would like to think I am pretty good, yet and still I found myself wondering if I were up for the task. I quickly came to the realization that I can do this. Who better for the job than me? I have known her many years. We have laughed together, cried together and worshipped together. I think about the countless hours spent reading, mulling over ideas and the two of us shedding tears not only of sorrow of loss but also tears of joy for the victories won. Spending that time with her allowed me to see her for more than a gifted dancer and amazing instructor but for her loving spirit and huge heart. She has a strength that draws people of all ages to her. Her ability to make you feel like family and her way of building you up when you are down is truly a gift from God above. What this author is doing is more than just writing a book and great story, but she is showing her readers just how precious life is, and that we may not be able to control what happens around us, but we can control how we react to those things that are not in our control. This book is based on real-life experiences and speaks to how the author not only faced enormous pain, but triumphantly and gracefully rose above and conquered her fears of the unknown.

I remember the moment I met the author. As I entered the dance studio of the large beautiful church, adults, teenagers and wee little children were milling around. Some were stretching their muscles; others were off to the side silently and inconspicuously practicing dance moves. Then a woman I now know was in her fifties but could have easily passed for years younger approached me. A lively woman, full of energy with a dancer's body, she blurted out "Hello, I'm bjai. You here to dance?" I quickly stated that I was only there to sign my teenage daughter up for dance and that I, myself, was not interested in dancing. "Come on!" she ordered. "You're dancing too." This feisty small woman with the thick New York accent has a gift of persuasion and now some 15 years later, we still dance together.

God has a way of placing certain people in your path that really change your life even though you may not realize it at the time. Sometimes those people are there for a lifetime and some people are with you for only a season. I am so blessed to have this author in my life for the long term. I pray our relationship continues to grow even though we live in two different states now. We will forever be connected through the power of dance and words. I pray her readers find peace, strength, and hope in the following pages. Read on and be blessed…

# Table of Contents

# BREATHE

# Introduction

Here I go again . . .

I started writing in a journal, but it was just too small.

Now that I think about it, is there a journal, a book, a pad, a tablet or even a computer large enough to hold *LIFE?*

My pastor instructs us not to talk about the mountain, but rather he tells us to speak to our mountain. Today, I need to talk to you about when there was a mountain. In fact, I need to talk to you about when there is an entire mountain range.

The circumstances I've dealt with over the last several months have turned my life totally upside down. I pray I'll never have to deal with anything like this again or have anyone I know deal with such circumstances. Yet:

I have seen the hand of my God move like I've never seen before.

I have experienced the love and support of family and friends like I've never experienced before.

I have seen my church and its leadership in a light that I've never seen before.

I am experiencing a peace I've never experienced before.

*Breathe*

Dear Reader,

Throughout this book, I have dedicated certain pages to you, my reader.

The purpose of my 'reader pages' is to pull away from the story and share my most intimate thoughts and feelings, at that very moment, and allow us a few seconds to just breathe.

I'd like to believe that on these pages, I might even address you and your situation or circumstances directly.

This is my first reader page.

bjai

# Chapter One

# August 3rd

Today is the beginning . . . well I suppose that's a paradox . . . today is the beginning of the month of August, August 3rd. Today is also the end of my life as I've known it.

Last night we turned off my honey's ventilator. My honey is my husband. His name is Buddy. Buddy held his own thru the night.

Father God has just wrapped me in His arms and covered me with a strength that I know is not from me, but a gift from the Lord. My prayer is that peace, the peace that can't be explained, settle in on our daughters Nicole, Michelle and Jolie. I pray this especially for my baby girl Jolie. She is really struggling at this moment.

She needs to release her Daddy and allow this peace to settle in and take over.

It makes me think back when she was a little girl and wouldn't let go. When a stranger would come to the house, Jolie would want to be in the room, but needing that safe place she'd grab her Daddy's leg and would hold on for dear life. She wasn't letting go as long as that present fear was around. She is holding on now, and it is time for my baby girl to let go.

# August 4th

My honey is still with us.

Nicole and Tony, my oldest daughter and son-in-law, were headed back to Maryland with my mom. My mom, who was 97 years old, was not very mobile due to age, but it was such a comfort just having her here with me.

Jolie has finally left the hospital and will be going home, back to northern Virginia, with her sister Michelle, whom I possessively call MyChell. They have all left. Now peace and solace can settle in . . . Today is my husband's opportunity for *Flight!!*

My crying is sporadic; the tears come without warning, very short bursts. I've never experienced anything like this before. I literally go from sobbing to smiling . . .

I feel a little crazy . . . whew, this is wearing me out . . . . I'm so very tired.

*Breathe

I decided to spend a quiet evening at the hospital with my husband. No nurses, no medical team, no prayer warriors, no pastors, no friends, and no family, tonight just us two . . . I dressed up and took

the jazz CD that MyChell made for us and closed the door. What an amazing night.

I sat by his bed and began reminiscing. "Honey, remember our wedding or rather, the day we got married? Nobody knew what was happening except our best friends, Bill and Weda. The week before, I shopped with my mom for my Easter outfit and Mom asked, "Why do you need a white Easter outfit? Isn't Easter supposed to be full of color?" She didn't have a clue, but this outfit was going to be my wedding outfit. You and I were eloping and I was so excited.

After we got married, you brought me home, and we had our traditional Sunday dinner with my family, and no one knew what we had done. I cringed as the uncooked wedding rice fell from my hair onto the empty china dinner plate. I can still remember how hard I prayed that nobody heard the "ping" of the rice. Then we both looked at each other and got so tickled, we couldn't stop laughing. I can hear my aunt Elsie saying "Young people today are just so silly."

You kissed me goodnight and left that night and every night for the next six months.

We had a secret no one knew but us. Just us.

I know you're about to leave me again and this time it's OK.

Well that evening I cried for the both of us; I danced for the both of us, and I laughed for the both of us. Together we enjoyed our last date night.

# Chapter Two

# August 5th

What an amazing experience. My honey is still with us.

Tonight Jackie & Rika Hobson, Judy & Buddy Adams, Katie Sandy and the Brian Family came to hang out with Buddy. We chatted and joked and just loved on each other. The room was filled with a light fragrance of love and warmth. We surrounded the bed and prayed, opening the door for the Holy Spirit to take over. Prayers came spontaneously as folks felt led to pray, then silence, a long, long thick silence . . . As I held tight to my husband's hand and Rika laid her hand on his chest, I began to thank God:

I thanked God for giving me fifty years, exactly fifty years and four months to spend with my husband, my wonderful life partner.

I thanked God for the awesome dad He allowed this man to become to our three girls.

I thanked Him for giving us the provider and the protector that He did in Buddy Clayburn.

Just as I finished with that final "Amen" I realized... no pulse and I looked up at Rika just as she realized . . . no heartbeat. Jackie reached over and gently closed his eyes, as if to close the curtain on this stage of life. I'd like to believe my honey was just waiting to hear my voice one more time before he left.   No more pain, and praise was in order. We filled that room with an attitude of rejoicing. He's gone . . . He's gone home.  Yes, my honey is now hanging with Jesus!

I witnessed the death certificate and left the corpse there because my husband, my love, my Buddy had already left the building.

Dear Reader,

Writing is hard, very hard.

It's hard to make you, the reader, understand and experience that feeling. Especially when "that feeling" is the product of conflicting emotions. When death brings both happiness and sadness it's hard to translate that from your head, from your heart onto a plain piece of paper.

Writing is hard, writing is very very hard...............

bjai

I went home that night and sat on my back porch with four lovely ladies: Jackie, Rika, Frieda, and Rethia. We told stories, laughed and cried together. It's midnight and I know my neighbors are wondering, "What's the party for? What's going on at the Clayburn house?" The entire neighborhood is totally silent except for my back porch.

Alright, it's late and I'm tired. Yes, I told everyone to go home! No one wanted to leave me. Everyone felt the need to care for me that night. But I was really alright. My family wanted to spend the night; Jackie planned to take the guest room, and Rika planned to take the sofa. I love my caring family & friends so much but:

"No, you may not spend the night. Go home. Please, go home."

I need to have this night alone, just me, I need this night and I need this time to Feel the moment. Tonight, it's going to be just me & Jesus.

LOVE NEVER DIES!

*Breathe

# August 6th

What am I going to do now?

It was just a couple of weeks ago we sat in the car for over two hours and talked about this growth on my breast. Dare we call it cancer? Was I that sick?

We hadn't seen a doctor yet, but we prayed, and we knew I'd be OK. I knew whatever the outcome Buddy and I could and would handle it together. In fact, several times prior to the last couple of days, we'd look at each other and one of us would say, "Whatever together"

*What am I going to do now?*

# Chapter Three

# July 22nd

# REFLECTING

I remember what a perfect day July 22nd was. It was warm, sunny and full of romping, giggling children. I sat in the swing hiding from my manic husband as he drenched the kids with the water hose. They ran for cover behind trees, rolled up and down the yard and screamed with joy whenever Buddy got close.

"Alright it's time for nap, let's go, gang," I yelled.

"And I'm about to mow the yard," replied my honey.

What a perfect day!

The kids were out of their bathing suits and in dry clothes and were finally settled down for nap when I heard Buddy call *"BJAI"*.

I remember, thinking back, *Is Buddy upset about something?* because his call would normally be, "Hey Booby".

As I entered the bedroom he was sitting on the side of the bed:

*Buddy:* I'm not feeling too good.

*Me:* So mow later, just lie down and rest for a minute.

*Buddy:* OK.

The call came again "BJAI".

"Honey, *Shhhh,* its naptime," I said, slightly agitated having just laid the children down.

*Buddy:* I think I need to go to the hospital.

*Me:* WHAT? *(I'm thinking, Weren't you just running up and down the yard not more than ten minutes ago?)* Alright, the kids are quiet. I'm going to run over to our neighbor and ask him to take you to the hospital, and I'll pick you up after the kids go home.

Before I can get out the door, once again I hear:

*Buddy:* "BJAI"

Did he not hear me ask him to be quiet?

Was he trying to wake the children?

*Me:* WHAT BUDDY?

*Buddy:* Call 911

And with an attitude shift, I answered:

*Me:* For real 911?

By the time the paramedics arrived my husband had to be carried out on a stretcher.

I recall being shocked at the look of desperation on Buddy's face.

His entire demeanor was very unfamiliar to me. It was one of total helplessness; I don't ever remember seeing Buddy in that physical state before.

Thinking back, I'll always wonder if my husband realized the seriousness of his condition. Maybe he knew something he didn't tell me.

I wonder if he realized that this would be the last time he would ever leave his home.

*\*Breathe*

# Chapter Four

# July 22nd

# AT THE HOSPITAL

His pain is unbearable . . . the pain medication is wearing off much too quickly, and it's very difficult to watch my husband suffer without any relief. He begs for me to help him, which leaves me feeling both helpless and useless. We are in the hospital; this is where you come to get help, right? I yell at doctors and nurses to no avail. They are doing all they can do.

Even when totally sedated, Buddy's body thrashes around in an attempt to deal with the pain. It is a nightmare.

I'm cold, I'm so cold. I'm not dressed for a night in the hospital. No, I am dressed for a summer day playing with the kids on my front lawn.

How did I get here? I'm so cold!

I called Jackie Hobson, and she and her daughter are on their way over. Thank God for family. The Hobsons are family. Now Jackie and Rika are here and they brought me a heavy sweater and a phone charger and support. Support is what really matters. They are with me and I am not alone.

I need to step out and walk for a minute. I've got a headache; I'm a little nauseous. The air seems thinner, and my breathing is slightly labored. I just need to walk. Walk and pray; yes, that's what I need to do. I'll just walk and pray.

As I walk the halls I notice how dark it is outside. Why is it so dark? It looks like winter.

Is it really one o'clock in the morning? That's why it's so dark. Have I been standing up for nine hours? Standing up for nine hours, in a cubby hole?

STOP. Let me evaluate this situation. Oh my goodness, Buddy is still in pain, nothing has changed except I'm cold, sick to the stomach, and tired of standing up.

Why the *HELL* aren't we in a room?

# AT THE NURSES STATION

They've asked me to lower my voice because it's one o'clock in the morning.

So I guess they do know what time it is?

"You've sedated my husband so he wouldn't disturb anyone at this late hour, now you better sedate me or give us a room" . . .

"No, I can't wait."


*Breathe

# July 23rd

OK, it's Wednesday.

What's happening here? Who do I call? What do I do?

Reverting to what I always do . . . Make a list:

- call the girls
- call the daycare parents
- call Tiff
- call Pastor

Cancel everything:

- Milk & Honey Daycare ...
- Ministry in Motion Dance...
- New Life VBS meeting ...
- New Life Harmony Dance practice...

Everything! Just cancel everything!

My focus now has to change.

Dear Reader,

There are times and situations that tend to throw everything into a state of confusion. Your intentions become muddled. Actions that were very clear yesterday now seemed lost in a screen of static.

Lord, help me focus!

bjai

There are certain things that can't be controlled or even explained. As a Christian, it was my desire to stay in control of my flesh, but the natural man is truly a peculiar being.

We are creatures of habit and tend to operate seeking a self-inflicted, 'destiny by design', attempting to plan our days, our weeks, our life out according to our own desires and our own visions.

So, when things began to fall apart and my calendar and my entire life became unfamiliar to me, not only confusion but frustration attempted to set in.

Right now, I'm feeling very out of control.

# August 7th

Click, Click, Click, Click, that should be the sound of "the turn off," Click, Click.

Maybe if I write it down I can turn it off . . . I so hate feeling dumb.

I'm standing in the bathroom trying to wake up and suddenly the alarm clock goes off.

*Oh, no,* I think. *Hurry up and turn it off before it wakes up Buddy. . . . WHAT??*

Yeah, I feel dumb!

Click, Click, turn off those crazy thoughts. *STOP IT!!*

I know Buddy's gone. Yes, Buddy is dead, but I can't seem to make my mind accept it.

Click Click turn off my mind – that's what I'm trying to turn off, but first turn off the damn alarm clock!

Confusion, yes, frustration and confusion had set in and with that came fear, fear of the unknown.

Fear of who I might become.

Fear of letting the outside change my inside.

Fear that life will change who I really am.

Will my past dictate my future?

Will these situations change the plans that God has for me?

Let me recapitulate.

Fourteen months ago, I buried my father. He was the first man that captured my heart.

Ten months ago, I suddenly lost my husband of fifty years, my soul mate, my provider, my protector . . . Gone!

Four months ago, I buried my mother.

In the middle of all the chaos, I was diagnosed with cancer.

Whew . . .

In the short time of about a year . . . I feel my total identity has changed. I've become someone else.

No longer a loving wife . . . I'm now a widow.

No longer a happy daughter . . . I'm now an orphan.

No longer a healthy and vibrant dancer . . . I'm now a victim.

Oh my GOD . . . I want to know who changed the channel? Who flipped the script?

My entire life as I had known it two years ago was turned inside out, upside down, shaken apart, and laid in front of me in shambles, and I can't pick it up, and I can't put it back together . . .

### *I CANNOT FIX THIS*

*Breathe

# Chapter Five

# August 1st

# THE DECISION

They called us in today to discuss options for my love. I really didn't think I wanted to do this, but I knew I had to, and I knew I had to take the lead.

I asked my pastors Tony & Sharon Atkinson to meet us there.

The medical team took their position at the table, facing our family, and the meeting began. As the doctors talked, I became disconnected and slightly irritated. I became almost breathless. I apologized for interrupting their medical rhetoric and asked them to excuse the fact that I was about to turn my back to them and address my family. They nodded cordially.

I braced myself against the conference table as I summoned the ability to speak with authority.

"I know you love your daddy. I know everyone in this room loves him, excluding the medical team. But know this: nobody in this room loves him more than I do. Nobody knows his heart's desires like I do. Please keep that in mind as I talk to you.

"I know my husband better than anyone else on this planet does. So, I say with total confidence . . . My husband will not stand for a compromised existence."

The doctors were very cooperative as I addressed them.

"If mobile, my husband will have to be on a ventilator and pull a canister around the rest of his life because he can no longer breathe on his own. Correct? "

They nodded with a quiet 'yes' . . . I responded "NO".

"He'll have to wear a colostomy bag because his bowels no longer work. Correct?"

They nodded 'yes' . . . I responded, "NO".

"He'll have to be dependent on a dialysis machine because his kidneys no longer work. Correct?"

Again, they nodded, 'yes' . . . I responded, "NO".

"And my husband, who would rather talk than eat, will have to live in a back room confined to a hospital bed for the rest of his life?

"No, No, and NO!" I tearfully but firmly stated.

"I put my dog down so he wouldn't have to suffer. I'll not make my man or let anyone else make him live like that. **NO!**

"I'm making the decision. and I pray to God you all understand, but . . . Shut him down."

The entire world seemed to stand still. Was anyone breathing? Motion resumed when our oldest daughter Nikki reached across the table for my hand in agreement with my decision. We began weeping together as she asked, "Are you sure, Mommy? Are you really sure?"

I confirmed my 'Yes' with a nod as I glanced around the room for approval from everyone else. Tears began to quietly fall from my baby girl Jo, my daughter MyChell, and my pastors.

Then the strength in the room, my son-in-law Tony, broke the silence with the shuffle of his clothes as he stood up and walked

over to me. He hugged me, and then firmly took my hand and almost lifted me from my seat as he began to talk. His firm grip and strong tone filled up every crevice in the entire room. At that moment, he truly was God-sent.

*My daughter Nikki and her husband, Tony.*

*'The strength in the room."*

I knew Tony loved me like the son I never had. He began to tell of the love he had for me and Pop, and had to hold back tears as he shared. He thanked me for having the strength to make this hard decision and said that he prayed that his wife would have that same tenacity if it was ever called for. He told me how proud he was to be my son-in-law. He truly took my breath away, and I wondered if Tony kept talking would I be able to continue breathing?

As I stood up, MyChell came up behind me and wrapped herself around me, as if to shelter me from any harshness. I remember feeling not only loved but protected and supported. I knew my girls had me.

My baby girl Jolie was dealing with the reality of losing her daddy. I think it might always be hardest on the youngest.

Pastor Sharron leaned over and held her as she cried.
The harshness of that day was cushioned by an unexpected revelation. As I started to leave the room, Buddy's doctor hugged me and whispered, "Normally at this stage, family members are screaming, crying and rolling around on the floor. The strength I see in this room has to be from a supernatural God. Thank you for sharing Him with us today."

Yes, Buddy's Muslim doctor was affected. I believe a seed was planted and something wonderful had happen in the midst of that horrific day.

Pastor Tony dried his tears, quietly said, "You know we're here for you," and he hugged me.

As they left, Pastor Sharon whispered in my ear . . . "Bjai Clayburn, I love you and you are my hero."

Hero? Is that really what she sees?

Could she not see my entire body shaking?

Could she not hear how loudly my heart was beating?

Could she not tell how badly I wanted to scream?

Could she not see how tightly I was clinging to Isaiah 41:10, trying not to fear or to become anxious?

Could she not see that I was trying with all that I had to totally depend on my God that promised to both love and strengthen me?

Hero, is that really what she sees?

Dear Reader,

There is a strength that can't be explained.

A strength that is summoned by faith.

A strength that rears up in a panicked mother to fight the bear for her baby.

A strength that moves a dad to enter the flames to save his son.

A strength that permits this wife to accept becoming a widow.

Thank you, Father, for blessing me with the promise of your word, in Isaiah 41:10.

> So do not fear, for I am with you; do not be dismayed,
> for I am your God. I will strengthen you and help you;
> I will uphold you with my righteous right hand.

A promise permitting me to walk in your supernatural strength, a strength that allowed me to do what was needed to be done in that room, on that day.

bjai

Chapter Six

# HOSPICE

The things you can learn in the oddest situations really amaze me.

Palliative.

Had I ever heard that word before?  To my knowledge I hadn't.

Palliative.

They asked me if they could place my honey on the Palliative floor. As a child my Mom would suddenly throw an unfamiliar word at me. Even if I don't know a word, I could usually figure out the meaning by hearing the context she used it in.

Not palliative.  I decided to look it up. I must be spelling it wrong, because two of the phrases in the definition I found were, "hospice care" and "no cure can be expected".   No, I didn't spell it wrong, nor was I really shocked.  I had already accepted all the facts and made all the needed decisions.

I can't explain why I was so stunned that they actually had a name for this type of care, an actual name for his care.  They had an entire hospital floor designated for my dying husband?  Well of course they did.  I'd just never had an occasion to think about it before.

Palliative care.

I suppose it was a good thing. The job of the entire staff was to make my husband comfortable and that was the goal my entire being was striving for. No more pain.

*Breathe

*Dear Reader*

*There are certain words that just can't be explained. They can't be significantly explained by you, me, or even Mr. Webster himself. Peace is one such word. Regardless of the dictionary definition, I tend to "feel" the scripture definition found in the book of Philippians. In chapter 4 verse 7 God promises a peace that surpasses any and all human understanding.*

> *And the peace of God, which transcends all understanding, will guard your heart and your minds in Christ Jesus.*

*That peace was the peace that stood guard over my heart and kept me in my right mind.*

*That peace was the peace that had me stand still when I wanted to run.*

*I don't know how I would have handled my situations without that amazing and comforting God-given peace.*

*bjai*

Certain things, certain events, leave a permanent imprint, a permanent picture in your mind.

Our oldest, Nikki, left in my mind an unforgettable mental video clip. After saying good-bye to her daddy, she began walking down the hall toward the waiting area, where we were all sitting. Her body looked artificially supported, as if an unseen force had slipped its hands under her armpits and was carrying her limp body. She covered her mouth with her open right hand, and she sobbed uncontrollably. Our youngest daughter, Jolie, attempted to comfort her sister, but was rejected. Nicole knew no comfort could ease the pain. She was unable to be comforted, unable to be hugged, and unable to be held by anyone, even her baby sister.

Fifteen months later, Nicole shared with me the fact she still felt bad that she did not have the ability to either receive or give comfort at that moment in the hospital hall, but if she had removed her hand from over her mouth, she said, she felt the entire hospital would quake with the magnitude of her screams.

Good-byes are difficult. Good-byes are so very difficult. Sometimes I think good-byes are easier for the one leaving then it is for the ones left behind, especially if the ones leaving are looking forward to their destination.

MyChell sat next to me, and her tears quietly washed her face.

After meeting with our doctors and the decision had been made, we all went back to Buddy's room. My husband did not appear to be coherent nor had he been able to communicate with us for several days. I leaned over his bed and told him about my decision to disconnect his ventilator. I told him I needed our children to know it was alright . . . No response. I asked him if he was ready to 'go home', to spend eternity with Jesus. No response. Nicole, standing at the foot of his bed said, "Daddy, don't worry; we got Mommy."

To the amazement of the entire room, including the medical team, Buddy looked at me and said, "I love you." I asked again, "Are you ready?" He responded with a thumbs up and said, "Yes I am" He was ready to go. Now was I ready to let him go?

*Breathe

Dear Reader,

I want you to know, that I pray this book speaks to your inner being, allowing you to know that you too can get through the struggle and come out victorious.

Thank you for taking the time to read my story.

bjai

# Chapter Seven

# August 9th

# HOME GOING

The celebration was amazing. My girls asked for no flowers, no tears, and no black. I looked around the church. It was an amazing sea of color. Hundreds of people—neighbors, friends and family—filled the five-hundred-seat church, and people were lining the walls. People began to approach us, sharing their love and condolences, sentiments, and encouraging remarks. Pastor Tony had to ask those standing in line to have a seat and wait until after service to greet us, otherwise we'd be there all night. Buddy had commanded a full house. In fact, it was standing room only. Pastor Sharon said, "In all the years and through all the services we seen, I've never seen anything like this one."

Nikki told the congregation how great they looked and that she believed her daddy, "Mr. Swag" himself, would really appreciate it. That service, we laughed at the stories about my husband; we cried at certain sentiments; we sang and even danced: yep I can truly say I danced at my husband's funeral (thanks to my Tiff, who called me out). We were reminded that our tears were selfish tears cause, as my daughter said, "Daddy wouldn't come back here with us if he could."

One of the most touching moments occurred when Cochise, an alumnus of Milk & Honey, our daycare, took the microphone and asked if everyone who came through our daycare would stand up. Oh my, I saw kids that I used to bottle feed, children whose diapers I used to change, and kids that Buddy carried around on his hip. They were now all grown up with families of their own. They had become pastors, policemen, parents, teachers, singers, and administrators. They were standing there, as if to say with that childish chant, "Look at me. Look at me. Hey Mrs. Bjai, Hey Mr. Buddy, look at me. Look what I did!!"

These grown men and women stood with their families and their tears summoned my tears . . . As I looked around the room, I thanked God for allowing us to be a part of their lives. I prayed that in all the years, through all things that we'd done, said, played, made, or sung, somewhere in the mix they got to see a glimpse of Jesus.

The military salute, the flag-folding, and being presented with the flag was a highlight of the service, as well as a true honor. What an amazing home going celebration.

# August 9th

# AT THE HOUSE

Jackie and my girls came home and took over the repast. They fed folks, loved on folks, and made sure everything was in place and flowing.

Meanwhile Rusty and Tiff were my quiet strength. Not a lot was said, but Rusty's hand on my shoulder as he passed by and the silent glances from Tiff spoke volumes. We are not related by blood, but we were joined at the heart, and they are family. Their support was priceless. This little Caucasian girl stepped into our lives, took up residence, and brought her husband Rusty with her. Buddy enjoyed 'messing' with waitresses, clerks, and unsuspecting strangers. As he'd refer to Tiff as one of his daughters, the response was priceless.

The Hobsons and I are only related by marriage, but if ever I could handpick a sister, she would have to be a 'Jackie Hobson.'

Her daughter Erika, my goddaughter, has affected my life tremendously. She touched my heart from the moment I first saw her, and she still does today. After the death of my honey, Jackie's husband Andrew made himself available to help me whenever needed. I love my family. They have been there from the beginning, and like the Daileys, I know they'll always be there. Jackie and Erika, along with Tiff and my girls, led the cleanup party. They stayed till the very end, and then sent everyone home.

# Chapter Eight

# After The Funeral

Now life starts *again*......

My girls became women on a mission.

They opened doors and windows, dumped drawers, cleaned out closets and cabinets, and with the help of their husbands, they even changed and rearranged bedrooms.

We would come across certain items and our emotions would rush in and overtake the moment. I remember sitting in the guest room looking across the hall into our bedroom, and Jolie lying on her Daddy's pillow quietly sobbing. I walked away and allowed her that time.

I've been told everyone handles their grief differently. I'm not sure if it was grief or the fact that for the first time in my life I was solely in charge of the finances, but I became very impulsive.

I paid off bills, closed accounts, paid off one car, and I bought myself a new car. But the most spontaneous thing I did was to buy a puppy. Yes, I bought myself a twelve-week-old puppy and named him Samson, after the biblical hero, and yes, he was my mighty warrior with a lot of hair. He became my shadow, my furry mate, my comfort. At two o'clock in the morning, he kept my feet warm, but I quickly cooled off at six o'clock in the morning when he had to go out. Did this dog really make me feel better? Yep, he absolutely did!

# Chapter Nine

# My Blessing: Our Three

You wonder, as parents, if you've raised your children to handle themselves the way you'd like them to in certain situations. After Buddy's death and funeral, I no longer worry about my girls. I now see them from a totally new perspective. My daughters are efficient, productive, decision-making women. They are women who are caretakers, problem solvers, motivators, need-meeters, and compassionate, faith-filled believers. Yet all three have totally different personalities and strengths. Buddy and I have been blessed to be the parents of three amazing women.

*This is a Christmas photo of MyChell and me that tells the story. I wasn't feeling 100% but Chell certainly was.*

That day in the conference room my girls took on a protective nature concerning my well-being, and it amazes me today that they still are my shield. My girls took me for infusions, injections, exams, and surgeries. I'm not sure if I could have gone through this successfully without them, but I know I made it because of them.

Let me tell you a little about my daughters. My middle daughter
MyChell held my hand during my very first chemotherapy infusion
and several after that. She sat by my bedside both in the hospital
and at home. She slept softly so she could get up at night if I was
in pain or even needed a drink of water.

MyChell was a tremendous help but there were things that did not
fit into her realm of support, such as nausea; that's right, nausea.
As I began to puke, my supportive daughter began to *run*. She
turned away from me, her needy mom; she covered her ears to
block my sounds and began to loudly sing a gibberish song. When
I could get my breath, we both looked at each other and began to
laugh hysterically.

*Whenever I'd come across this dance photo of
Nikki I'd smile because it always made me think
of that day she extended her hand from behind the
curtain wanting to ease my pain*

Nikki, my oldest, my
accomplished dancer,
held my hand as they
removed thirty-two
staples from my chest.
However, this tower
of strength held my
hand from behind a
curtain. Wanting to
be there for me, she
insisted on coming to
my appointment. As
I lay on the table, she
hid behind a dressing
curtain, stuck her hand
out and patted me on

the head, much like she was petting a puppy. As they removed my staples, she'd periodically ask, "Are you ok, Mom?" She couldn't bear to look, but she could ask.

Her fear was my pain.

My youngest, my baby girl Jolie, worked for a doctor and became one of my medical consultants. As the mother of my 16-year-old grandson, she was not able to make trips to Roanoke nearly as often as her sisters. We talked frequently, and if she didn't know the answer to a question I had, she'd

*My Jolie: always there for her Mommy.*

find out. I know it concerned her not to be with me as often as she wanted, but I knew she was always there in spirit and would definitely be there if I ever needed her. I remember for my very first solo doctor's appointment, I stopped to get gas and as I pulled away from the gas pumps, I became very emotional, very unsteady. I pulled into an empty parking space, called Jolie, and began to sob into the phone. At that moment, we switched roles. I became a child again, and she became the woman in charge.

Jolie talked me through that morning and made everything alright again.

# Chapter Ten

# THE VOICE OF REASON

Our God loves us so much.  He places certain people in our lives whose specific purpose is to meet a particular need, people in place to minister to us.  For that moment, for that season, I feel like they are God's angels on assignment.

That's how I viewed the entire Oshoniyi family: Melissa, her husband Toye, and their precious daughter Jaylen (whom I affectionately call Scrunch).  I look back over this last year and see many areas and many times this family has affected my life. I remember the day I was going to my first ultrasound.

Melissa insisted on going with me. Her reasoning was, as she said, "I'm in that area all the time and I know exactly where you need to go."

We chatted and laughed on the drive to the appointment.  We arrived outside a small apartment-type building, with a Yin Yang sign hanging on the outside instead of a medical shingle.  I had no idea that I wasn't going to a hospital or some sort of a medical facility. I thought, *This is a little strange.*

Inside, a gentleman led us to a tiny room, sort of a living room/office setting.  There was a floral sofa, a couple of chairs, a narrow table, and a desk.  It was not very sterile-looking. The man introduced us to his wife. She was a stout woman with long, straight blonde hair, dressed in a long multi-colored maxi skirt and a bell-sleeved blouse. She looked like an Elton John fan. The entire scene transported me back to the 70's, the hippie era, and yep, flower children. She spread a crisp white sheet across the narrow table.

Melissa left the room, assuring me, "I'll be right here, outside in the hall, Bjai."

I wonder now, if that reassurance was for me or was it a threat to our flower lady.

The woman told me to strip from my waist up and lie down on the table. It was necessary for the ultrasound, but it made me feel a little uncomfortable and very vulnerable. The examination was very painful as she applied pressure to my breast. She had to stop the ultrasound several times due to the intense pain. I closed my eyes, gritted my teeth and held my breath so she could get these photos done, when suddenly I was shocked. She went crazy. She fell across my nude body crying uncontrollably as she held me tightly . . . I thought, *Oh, my goodness, what is happening here? What did she see on these pictures?*

She began to sob. "My mother just died with *cancer*. I'm so sorry . . . I'm just so sorry . . . Please forgive me for crying . . . I'm so sorry."

I started thinking, *Sorry for what? Please stop crying and tell me what you're sorry for. Sorry you hurt me? Sorry you couldn't get a good picture? Sorry I've only got till the end of this week to live? Sorry? Sorry for what?*

Did she say cancer? That was the first time I had actually heard the word associated with me. CANCER! The word was actually released into the air. Now we're both crying. OK, please stop, please move, get off me, please let me up, and let me out. I want to run.

I wiped my face and tried to conceal my emotion as I walked toward the car. "Bjai, are you OK?" Melissa asked.

I nodded. I got in the car and started to drive. I silently drove as Melissa periodically gave directions. I could feel my emotion slowly growing to the point of explosion. As I pulled into my driveway I began to erupt.

Melissa asked, with a determination to not be pacified, "What is going on?"

At that moment, I erupted. We sat in the driveway, and I proceeded to tell her about my experience in that little room, with the crazy hippie.

I lost it. Poor Melissa tried so hard to reel me back in before I went to *that* place. It was too late. I talked about my cancer. I talked about getting an in-home nurse to care for me. I even talked about selling my home and moving to northern Virginia, maybe moving in with my daughters. Actually, I didn't really talk. I think it was more ranting than talking.

Then Melissa, providing a voice of reason, spoke up and brought me back to a safe place. "Bjai," she said in a firm but calm voice, "that woman is only a technician. She is trained to turn that machine off and on, and at best she is an amateur photographer. She can't even read and sign-off on the information she collects. She must send everything, every single picture, to a qualified doctor. She is only a technician who is trained to turn that machine off and turn that machine on. She is also a very unprofessional technician."

*Breathe

# Chapter Eleven

# POWERFUL

Alright, I'm back at that place again, and I'm asking the same question *again*.

What am I going to do now?   It's just me; it's not the "whatever, together team" anymore.  It's just me. Me versus cancer. Possibly the biggest battle of my life stands in front of me, and I may have to fight it alone. I know family and friends love and have compassion for me, but they just went through the death of Buddy with me. Can they handle anything else?  Can I handle anything else?

OK that was my pity party . . . and it's over.

A favorite minister of mine used to say, "You can be pitiful or you can be powerful, but you can't be both."

I looked at my crisis; then looked at my Christ, and I knew I must make a decision . . . I knew my God had a plan for my life.  I knew I had to fight for my destiny.  I now had to make up my mind that the trial was not about a feeling, even though the feelings were consuming at times.  It was about a decision.  I had a job to do.  I had a feat to accomplish.  I had to overcome the plan of the enemy. I knew that the victors' walk was on purpose, and so I told myself every morning as I sat on the edge of my bed, often in tears, "Bjai, shoulders back, head up, and strut. Today I will walk the victors' walk. I can't back up; I can't back down, and I can't give in."

So I decided. I decided to be POWERFUL!!

I believed this cancer was an attack against me, a very personal attack. I knew it would take a conscious effort to stand strong against the ploy that Satan had set into motion against me. I couldn't choose what came into my life but I could choose how I handled it. I put everything aside and began to spiritually arm myself.

- I took my pastor's healing classes.
- I studied healing scriptures.
- I checked my conversation and insisted those around me check theirs.
- I insisted that people became responsible for what they brought into my environment.
- Above all, Jesus became my constant.

In response to our prayers, the Master placed a hedge of love, support, and protection around me. He sent friends and neighbors to me who brought peace, solace, love, and encouragement into my world. These people were there any day, any time I had a need. In fact, even when I didn't have a name, they were still there. There were so many people that supported me, it would be impossible to mention them all. However, two vessels that the Master handpicked just for me were Veronica and Kay.

Veronica, a cancer survivor, is one of the lawyers that my oldest daughter, Nikki, worked for, a woman I've never seen, never met personally, yet she supported me from afar. She emailed me; she contacted me via my daughter; she even took the time to hand write me a letter. Veronica inundated me with both suggestions and information. I truly appreciated her input and was humbled by her concern for me, a virtual stranger.

Kay, a member of my church, stepped in my path the moment she found out I had breast cancer. Kay, being a cancer survivor herself, became my lighthouse in the storm. I began to look for her every Sunday morning. We didn't have to talk about anything specific. I just needed to see her. She was a strong, healthy wife, mother, and a high school basketball coach. Both of these ladies became my focus at two o'clock in the morning when Satan's whispers became deafening and fear tried to creep in. I knew that if my God could take them from the surgical table to the vibrant vision of health that they are now, I knew He not only could but He would do it for me.

Veronica and Kay made me aware that when going somewhere new for the first time, it's always helpful to get direction from someone who knows the route, has been there, and can tell you the hazards to avoid, the detours, and the ins and outs of the journey ahead. For me, my GPS, my compass, my order of direction were Veronica and Kay.

Other vessels, used by the Master, included the Dents, Pastor Richard, and his wife Rethia. I feel like I raised this couple along with my own children.

Richard would stick his head in the back door and holler "Bjai, throw me your car keys." I would and he'd disappear. An hour later he'd toss the keys back on the kitchen cabinet and leave.

When I'd get in my car I'd notice it was not only washed and filled up with gas, it was also detailed. There were times I'd wake up to my puppy barking at the noise outside, I'd peek out the window and there was Richard, gloves and boots on, hood up, scraping the snow and ice off my walkway. He never said a word, just did what he came to do then left. That Christ-like witness spoke louder than any words or any sermon he could have preached.

Pastor Richard's wife Rethia, being a nurse and a hospital employee, knew the hospital and its protocol inside and out, and she was there so much of the time, it allowed me the comfort of talking to her whenever I wanted to or whenever I needed to. Yet sitting here at this very moment in time, I can't remember a question I asked her or even a single conversation we had. But I'll always remember and I'll never be able to thank her enough for her last interaction concerning my husband.

As she entered Buddy's room, Rethia placed her hands firmly on the metal side rails of Buddy's bed, and as she spoke she seemed to shake the bed with the sound of her voice. "Buddy, Buddy, look at me! Do you hear me? Look at me, Buddy! Do you know who I am? Do you know who I am, Buddy? Do you know my name?"

Not wanting to exert any energy or experience her momentary harshness, my honey attempted to turn away. As he did, Rethia raised her voice with an uncomfortable determination.

"Buddy Clayburn, look at me," she said in a deep, harassing tone. "What's my name? I said, what's my name, Buddy?"

Stress began to form like a huge ball in the very pit of my belly, and it began to slowly rise into my throat. I felt as if I were going to choke, literally *choke*.

My husband's discomfort was very visible. Could she not see it? Of course, she had to see that. Why was she being so aggressive? No, why was she being so callous?

For the first time in over 20 years, I became angry with Rethia Dent. Not disturbed, not annoyed, not frustrated, not irritated, I became *angry* with Rethia Dent.

I remember how sensitive everything felt in the room at that moment. The instruments seem to take on a low rattle; her voice seemed to reverberate off the walls, and even the air seemed extremely heavy, weighty, almost tangible.

My husband was lying helpless on what was to be his deathbed. I felt obligated to intervene. Then, it happened.

My husband, whose voice I hadn't heard in days, out of sheer frustration, spoke. "Rethia," he uttered with eyes closed.

She looked at me and we both smiled, then she said, "Buddy, what did you say? I didn't hear you Buddy, What's my name?"

Again, my husband clearly said, "Rethia."

That anger in my stomach, that huge ball in my throat, melted into tears. Rethia had allowed me to hear Buddy's voice one more time and I knew he was still in there.

Dear Reader,

There is a way that seems right to us, but the end is merely the way of death. I pray you have someone that will speak life into your situation, even if that life is just for a fleeting moment. I pray you have someone who loves you enough to do what needs to be done, yet allow you room to just breathe.

bjai

# Chapter Twelve

# HEDGE OF PROTECTION

There was one specific incident which confirmed I had a hedge of protection in place that I could rely upon.

I had developed a cough and had a morning appointment to see my doctor about it. As always, I turned my phone down while in the medical appointment. Dropping my phone in my pocketbook, I accidently dialed Wanda's number. Wanda is a concerned neighbor that I had not spoken to in a couple of days. Wanda answered the phone, only to hear me coughing uncontrollably in the doctor's waiting room. She later told me she called my name several times and when I didn't answer she envisioned me lying in an alley in the throes of an asthma attack, unable to respond to her voice. Fearful of losing our connection, she refused to hang up her phone, but called the police department from another phone. They immediately started searching for me. After the doctor's appointment, I went grocery shopping, stopped and had breakfast, and then went and had my car serviced all while the police were frantically looking for a helpless old woman lying in the gutter suffering from an asthma attack. Once located and stopped by the patrolling police, I knew from that moment on my hedge of protection was definitely in place.

# Chapter Thirteen

# THE HONESTY OF CHILDREN

We own and operate a small daycare and many times the wisdom
in the house comes from the innocence and the honesty of the
children. We sometimes cook at our daycare. Last week we decided
to make a cake. Then it happened: human desire took over.

One of our young students, Sydney, wanted to use two teaspoons
of flour in our cake and four cups of sugar because, she said, "It's a
cake, and cakes are supposed to be sweet."

Rossi decided he didn't want to put eggs in our cake because "Eggs
are for breakfast, and they're not really for cake."

Jalen giggled as he suggested bacon, his favorite food.

Jaylen wanted to put a purple popsicle in our cake because she loves
popsicles and her favorite color is purple.

With their limited wisdom they were operating on their likes and
dislikes. They were operating on their own knowledge base. It all
made perfect sense to them; after all it was what they wanted, and it
even sounded good. Yes, it all made perfect sense.   But I knew the
end from the beginning.  I knew what the cake is supposed to look
like.  I knew what a cake is supposed to taste like.  If I gave them
what they thought they wanted, they'd be disappointed and they'd
have a mess.

I could see the mess before it was ever evident to those involved. In order to see success, the children had to submit to authority. Much like them, we tend to operate on our own knowledge base. We operate on what makes sense to us, or on what we want or what sounds good or looks good or feels good. We must also learn to submit to our heavenly Father's authority. He sees the mess before it's ever evident to us. He knows the plans He has for us. He knows the end from the beginning. We must learn to submit to God's authority in order to see His success in our lives. There is a proverb I like whose gist is, 'There is a way that seems right to us, but the end therefore is a mess." When we pray we think we know what we want. We think we know what we need. We pray according to our knowledge. Let me tell you our human knowledge tends to be lacking.

Thank you, Father, that You see the end from the beginning.

Thank you, Father. I can rest in the fact You know the end from the beginning concerning our lives.

Thank you, Father, that you know how to get us on the road to our perfect destiny.

Chapter Fourteen

# January 1st

# THE NEW YEAR

The New Year arrived. I got to move out of the old and into the new. Was that a good thing? Of course it was; I got to celebrate the future, celebrate the new beginnings. I'd made up my mind to do more than just survive. I'd decided to thrive. I was ready to move powerfully forward. I was done with the heartbreak, the loss, the suffering, done with the pain of last year . . . Just done.

Then, suddenly I felt like I'd just hit a cement wall. I experienced something I'd never felt before. I felt an extremely deep sense of loss at the thought of leaving. "Leaving what?" I asked myself.

My daughter Nicole called me that night and we cried together on the phone. She said, "Mommy, I knew you were feeling some kinda way tonight."

I told her that I was aware my feelings made absolutely no sense. Buddy died four months ago. Why now? Why did I feel like this now?

With the voice of clarity, my daughter simply said, "You feel like this because you're leaving Daddy."

"Leaving Daddy," I responded. "Leaving him where?" (I know she knows he is dead.)

"Mommy, you are leaving Daddy in last year," she replied.

So I rolled over and sobbed that night. And in the morning, I had entered a brand-new year, alone. But I knew I was going to be OK.

I prayed, "Lord I need to see You with new eyes. I knew my perspective, my boundaries. My vision must now change."

My life has been altered. I must now become more than I've ever been. So my prayer was, "Lord grant me a bigger vision and the ability to fulfill that vision." And like Solomon, I prayed for both knowledge and wisdom. Just when I had made the decision, or if you would have it, made a resolution, a New Year's resolution that I was on my way to having everything God said I could have, *I was sucker punched!*

# February

# MOM

Nicole called this morning after talking to MyChell. "Mommy, Nana is in transition," she said.

*What transition?* I asked myself. *Does she mean my mother is dying? It hasn't been that long ago since I buried my daddy.*

*Please, Lord, not now; please not now.*

I certainly didn't see this coming. I must have blinked. I felt like I'd been slapped.

Due to my illness, the distance, and MyChell's availability, the hospital called her. She got the news while she was at work. She was heartbroken. Her confident, her shield, her Nana . . . gone. In her office she lost it, she lost her composure.

Her co-worker came in to check on her, asking, "Are you alright Michelle?"

She shook her head 'no' and—speechless—she wrote, "My Nana died. I'm going home." on a piece of paper and she left.
What's that old saying? Bad news comes in threes. My husband,

cancer, my parents: maybe I should apply to be the poster child for *that* rule? I think the word 'surreal' fits here. I felt as if I was in a place between fantasy and reality. Did I question God? Yes, I did. It's an oxymoron, but I questioned because of my certainty. I was certain that the word of God was true. I was certain He was in control. I was certain that the Word said God wouldn't put more on me than I could tolerate. But maybe, just maybe He got confused. Maybe He got me mixed up with someone else; someone stronger, someone with more stamina, and more faith. Did I question God? Yes I did, but only for a minute. Then I checked myself. I didn't know if I was strong enough to take another blow but I had made the decision to be powerful and I was not going to be swayed off that decision. Most of the time you don't know if you are strong enough, until being strong enough is your only option. I will be powerful and walk out God's plan for my life; I will walk the victors' walk because I am my mother's daughter. Strong willed, determined and a 'get the job done' kind of woman . . . that was my mom!

*My mommy*

Dear Reader,

There were so many things, so many important details I wish I had known. Things I think every person sharing life together with someone else needs to know. My life would have been so much easier if I had known what to do before I was thrust into this turmoil. Grieving had to take a back seat to the immediate demands of the moment.

These are things I think every person sharing life together with someone else needs to know:

Insurance:

What am I expected to do?
Who am I expected to contact?
Do they know Buddy died?

Car:

Where are the titles?
Are the titles in my name?
Can I sell his car?
Does the oil need to be changed?
Does the car need brakes?
What in the world does a tune up actually do?

Bills:

Where do I pay the mortgage?

Am I responsible for Buddy's bills?

Will they turn my electricity off and leave me sitting in
the dark without contacting me?

How do I light the fireplace?

Taxes: Who should I contact?

Who'll cut the grass, and plant the flowers?

Who will be my Buddy? Who will do his job? I guess I will.

I had no idea the fight that was ahead.

I fought with the cable company.

I fought with the bank.

I fought with the DMV.

I fought with the hospital.

Just to name a few, and no, I didn't win every fight but I came
out stronger each and every time.

bjai

*Post script:*

*My prayer for you, Dear Reader, is that, you be the one in charge and not allow life situations to dictate your direction.*

*My prayer is that you realize and accept that you are not free from the battles, but you are free to win.*

# Chapter Fifteen

# March

There are things that you know that you know. Things no one can change your mind about and you can't be convinced or persuaded otherwise. For example; my name is Bjai. Even if you don't like the name or if you insist on calling me Sally, *I know that I know* that my name is Bjai.

There are things that you know that you know like:

>    Your address
>
>    Your phone numbers
>
>    What you ate for breakfast
>
>    If you have a driver's license.

Because you know that you know these things, you can't be persuaded differently.

I'm about to suit up for battle. My armor and my ammunition will be the things "I know" in my Spirit.

So, let me tell you what I KNEW:

I knew that I knew when the craziness set in and everything was upside down, that there was at least one thing stable in my life and it was JESUS!

I knew that I knew He didn't have to prepare or get ready for me. He didn't have to develop a plan of action.

I knew that I knew He didn't have to think about it because I was *always* on His mind.

I knew that I knew He was not thrown, shocked, taken aback, or floored by my situation.

I knew that I knew He was my refuge, my comfort, and my strong tower.

I knew that I knew He had given His angels charge over me.

I knew that I knew God would hold me tight and not let go no matter how chaotic the ride.

I knew that I knew He sent His son to that cross not only for my iniquity, my sin, but also for my infirmities, my sickness.

I knew that I knew that one of those stripes my Jesus took was for *cancer.* And it was only in Him that I could trust.

I knew that healing was not an addendum to the contract but it was part of the package, part of the salvation package. If I could be saved, then I could be healed. I was experiencing my Savior on a totally new and different level. I was letting God be God; He was so much better at it then I was. I was getting to know Him in a more intimate way. I now had an increased knowledge and a greater manifestation of His love for me. My inner being had truly been changed.

Pastor Sharon said to me last week, "Lady there's something different about you."

I was shocked. I didn't think anyone could see the change, but I agree with her: I am not the same person I was last year. Many of us can look back and point to a situation or an event that affected our lives. But what I'm talking about is different. This was not an event or a situation. This was a journey; an entire journey that not only affected but changed my entire being. Much like the difference between being pregnant and actually having a child: one being an event that lasts for a season, while the other changes your life forever. The difference was so pronounced that it had become physically evident. I'd had a divine encounter with God and yes, I was a different person.

He who created this universe, He who holds the waters of the worlds in the palm of His hand, my maker, had been magnified in my spirit. He, who rotates this massive creation and places the stars in the sky, *He* knows my name. *He* touched my life . . . How could I not be changed?

I have been through the fire and I don't smell of smoke. I have been through the waters and I did not drown. How could I not be changed?

Of course I was.

Dear Reader,

I wrote my story because of an enormous need to get it out. Not necessarily a need to get it out into the hands of the public, but a need to get it out into the air: I needed to get it out of me.

We all have a story to share or a story to tell, a story that might touch this universe.

In sharing my story, I may not have changed the world, but it has changed me.

I have come to the realization that I don't get to choose what comes into my life, but I certainly do get to choose how I handle it.

bjai

# Chapter Sixteen

# SOAPBOX

Please allow me a moment to climb on my soapbox.

During this journey I have encountered many different people, with many different ideas concerning my situation, but one of the amazing thought processes is the Christian belief system.

I'm not sure whether we actually believe what we believe because of peer influence or because of knowledge. Maybe our beliefs are generated because of a specific need in our own lives or maybe because of what we've seen or experienced rather than on the word of God? Is our spiritual foundation based on the latest bestseller, or is it based on the leading of the Holy Spirit? Is what we know and believe purchased off the 'up and coming' new author shelf in the Christian book store?

Can we stop acting like our faith will ward off the trials of this world? The Word says it will rain on the just and the unjust. We, as Christians, feel the need to perform not only for the world, but for each other. Our trials do not speak to the power, the magnitude, or viability of our faith.

Know that our faith will not keep us from the tribulations of life, but our faith will work differently for us than for those in the world.

My trials have made me stronger and productive. For the unbeliever, trials become a heavy weight, destructive and non-productive. My trials became a stepping stone on a designated journey to a called destiny. We pray "Lord, help me. Lord, fix my tongue, cleanse my mouth." That's wonderful, but can we go a little deeper? Can we focus on our hearts, because out of the abundance of our heart, our mouth speaks? Can we fix the root?

The battle is not always between us and the world. Sometimes it's just between us and ourselves. We allow the natural to nullify our faith in the supernatural. We let our body speak to us. We let the pain and the hurt speak to us

The darkness speaks to us. The medical test speaks to us.

We have to stop it! Faith is not the seen but the unseen (Hebrews 11:1).

Anybody can call it what it is. We need to call it what God calls it.

It says in Psalm 139:14 that our bodies are "fearfully and wonderfully" designed, with overcoming power.

In Deu.7:15, we are told that sickness should be far from us. God says He will not abandon us and He will make our path known to us and His presence will be our joy.

In Proverbs 3:5-6 God has told us that even in the darkness we don't have to lean on our own understanding. He will be the lamp that directs our path.

Let's grow up, family. Don't consider the trial but rather consider the promise!

We have the very mind of Christ. Wisdom and knowledge are our way of life. There is not a weapon formed on earth or in hell itself that can prosper against us. We are divinely healed from all mental, spiritual, or physical shortcomings that the enemy might attempt to lay on us. We rule and reign with dominion over the enemy.

We are whole and complete in the name of Jesus. Nothing missing and nothing broken.

Life's circumstances will not make me change who I am. My question today is, "Who are you?"

# STRAPPED

Bottom line: I knew that my God was not only God on the mountaintop, when Buddy and I sat at the dining room table laughing uncontrollably. I knew that my God was also my God in the valley, when I stood at Quantico at my husband's gravesite.

I knew as my body was being infused with chemicals during chemotherapy, and as I was being disfigured on that surgical table, and I knew as they exposed me to deadly radiation. I knew my God was still God.

Yes, He is God on the mountaintop, but yes, He is God in the valley. He is God who will show himself strong on your behalf, just as He did for me. Again, I just knew that I knew, and I couldn't be convinced or persuaded otherwise.

So look out, Satan. I'm strapped and I'm locked and loaded and ready for the battle!

I started this book by saying, "We've been instructed not to talk about our mountains but rather to speak to our mountains." Well, as you've read, I have talked to you about my mountains, *but hear this:*

My Daddy, God, girded me up and came around behind me, and

He supported my back as I leaned on Him. He pushed me up that mountain.

When I was totally worn out and thought, *No more, no further. I just can't do this,* He stepped out in front of me and took my hand and pulled me up that mountain.

And when I began to count the steps, Oh My God, so many steps, My Daddy came alongside of me, put His arm around my shoulders and walked and talked with me, and it was then I could almost tangibly feel His strength. I could smell His breath. It was then I could rest my head on His shoulder, and it was then I could hear His heartbeat . . . Mountain . . . What mountain?

**NOT TODAY, SATAN, NOT TODAY!**

Dear Reader,

This will be my final 'reader page'.

I have moved from information to revelation, so I thought I'd share with you a few lessons I've learned. While traveling on this journey through my life, there were things I knew but now, those things, I've realized.

*Satan may take me down, but he will not take me out (unless I give him permission).

*My outside does not have to contaminate my inside (unless I let it).

*Weeping may come for a season but joy does follow (if I allow it).

God has placed an awesome power in my hands, my testimony, and I will use it to bring Glory to his name.

bjai

# We love you ♡

Faith is not about *'it'* being OK.

Faith is about knowing you'll be OK,

no matter how *'it'* turns out.

# About the Author

## Brenda (bjai) Clayburn

Brenda (bjai) Clayburn was born in Norfolk VA., but bred in New York from the age of eleven months old.

The Clayburn's with their three daughters returned to VA. to work with children in the school system, eventually establishing 'Milk & Honey' pre-school. Holding the position as a Children's pastor and the owner/director of Ministry In Motion dance troupe, life was fun, full, and busy until, the script was flipped.

Allow this book to help you work through your situations:

From the valley to the mountain top.

From the test to the testimony. Just . . . "Breathe"

Made in the USA
Middletown, DE
16 June 2021